POSTCARDS · FROM ·

China

Zoë Dawson

RSVP

RAINTREE
STECK-VAUGHN
P U B L I S H E R S
The Steck-Vaughn Company

Austin, Texas

Published by Raintree Steck-Vaughn Publishers, an imprint of Steck-Vaughn Company

A ZOË BOOK

Editor: Kath Davies, Helene Resky
Design: Jan Sterling, Sterling Associates
Map: Gecko Limited
Production: Grahame Griffiths

Library of Congress Cataloging-in-Publication Data

Dawson, Zoë.
    China / Zoë Dawson.
        p. cm. — (Postcards from)
    Includes index.
    ISBN 0-8172-4007-1 (lib. binding)
    ISBN 0-8172-4228-7 (softcover)
    1. China — Description and travel — Juvenile literature.
    [1. China — Description and travel. 2. Letters.] I. Title. II. Series.
    DS712.D387 1996
    951–dc20
                                                                        95–8099
                                                                            CIP
                                                                             AC
Printed and bound in the United States
11 12 13 14 15 16 WZ 04

Photographic acknowledgments

The publishers wish to acknowledge, with thanks, the following photographic sources:

The Hutchison Library / Stella Martin - cover tl; / John Egan - title page, 22; / Mischa Scorer 6; / Melanie Friend 8; / Christine Pemberton 10; / R. Ian Lloyd 14; / René-Nicholas Guidicelli 18; / Felix Greene 24; Robert Harding Picture Library / Alain Evrard - cover bl; Impact Photos / Christophe Bluntzer 26, 28; Zefa - cover r, 12, 16, 20.

The publishers have made every effort to trace the copyright holders, but if they have inadvertently overlooked any, they will be pleased to make the necessary arrangement at the first opportunity.

Contents

All the words that appear in **bold** are explained in the Glossary on page 30.

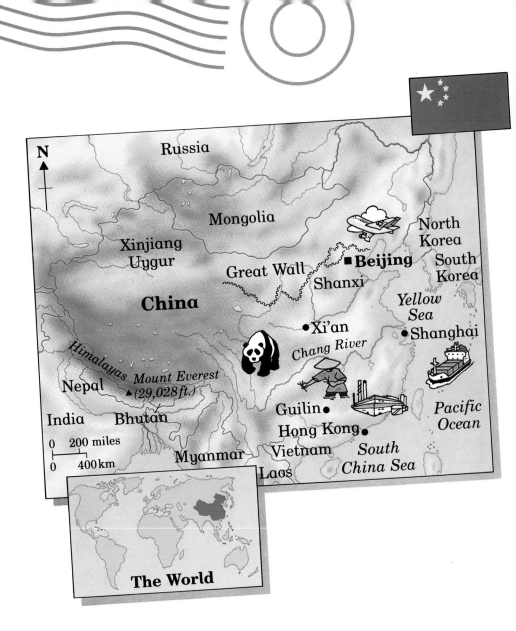

A big map of China
and a small map of the world

Dear Alice,

China is a long way from home. The plane took 16 hours to fly here from Los Angeles. You can see China in red on the small map. It is the third biggest country in the world.

Love,

Sharon

P.S. Mom says that more than one billion people live in China. More people live here than in any other country.

One of the main roads in Beijing

Dear Tim,

We are in Beijing. It is the **capital** of China. Most people here ride bikes to get around the city. We got on a bus. We paid with Chinese money called *renminbi*.

Love,

Asa

P.S. Dad says that Beijing is not the biggest city in China, but it is the most important one. Beijing has been the capital of China for more than 800 years.

Eating out in Beijing

Dear Liz,

We went out for dinner last night. We had bowls of rice, pieces of duck, and a sauce made with beans. People in China do not use knives and forks. We ate our food with **chopsticks** and a spoon.

Love,

Tanya

P.S. Dad says that people cook in different ways in China. In the north people eat noodles or bread. In the south they eat rice.

In the Forbidden City, Beijing

Dear Sanjay,

Long ago, the **emperors** who ruled China lived in this part of Beijing. Other people were not allowed in. That is why it is called the Forbidden City.

Love,

Mia

P.S. Mom says that the emperors were called the "Sons of Heaven." They came to pray in this **temple**. It is called the Temple of Heaven.

A steam locomotive in Shanxi

Dear Beth,

Most people in China do not have cars. Many people travel long distances by train. **Steam locomotives** like this one are built in Shanxi. They can pull heavy trains.

Love,

Amy

P.S. Mom says that most cities in China are far apart. Train trips take a long time. It is much quicker to fly. There are not many trucks on the roads because **goods** are sent by train.

The Great Wall of China

Dear Gianni,

People started to build the Great Wall across the north of China more than 2,000 years ago. It was about 6,000 miles (9,650 km) long. It took more than 1,000 years to build.

Love,

Alex

P.S. Dad says that the Great Wall was built to protect China from its enemies to the north. Today about 1,500 miles (2,400 km) remain. You can see the Great Wall from the moon!

The terra-cotta army, Xi'an

Dear Ellie,

These soldiers look real, but they are not. They are made out of **clay** called **terra-cotta**. There are thousands of soldiers in the terra-cotta army.

Love,

Nickie

P.S. Mom says that the terra-cotta army was made about 2,000 years ago. The army guarded the **tomb** of the first emperor of China. The clay soldiers were buried with the emperor.

Boats on the Chang River

Dear Emily,

This is one of the longest rivers in the world. It flows from the mountains in Tibet across China to the sea. Boats called *junks* carry people and goods along the river.

Love,

Harriet

P.S. Dad says that the highest mountain in the world is in Tibet. Tibet is a cold and beautiful place. Many people who live there do not want to be ruled by the Chinese.

The Chang River at Shanghai

Dear Lewis,

Shanghai is the biggest city in China. There are ships from all over the world in the harbor. A few people here speak English. Most people speak only Chinese. Chinese writing looks like pictures.

Love,

Jessie

P.S. Dad says that more than 13 million people live in Shanghai.

Fishing boats on the Gui Jiang River, Guilin

Dear Karen,

It is warm and wet here in southern China. Many **tourists** come to Guilin to see the country. It looks just like the old Chinese paintings we saw in Beijing.

Love,

Tracey

P.S. Most of the farmers here grow rice and tea. Mom says that these **crops** are often sent by boat to the cities in the north.

Tai chi in the Forbidden City, Beijing

Dear Gary,

We have seen lots of people in China do tai chi exercises every day to stay fit. The Chinese are good at many sports, such as swimming, basketball, and table tennis.

Your friend,

Pete

P.S. Dad says that people have done tai chi in China for thousands of years. Tai chi is as old as kung fu, which comes from China, too.

The Uygur in Xinjiang dressed up
for Chinese New Year.

Dear Helen,

People in China have short vacations. The most important holiday is in the spring at Chinese New Year. Some people dress up and dance in the streets for this **festival**.

Love,

Laurie

P.S. Mom says that most Chinese festivals are very old. The dates for them are set by the position of the moon. This means that they are held on different days each year.

The Chinese flag

Dear Richard,

The red on the flag stands for the Chinese **revolution**. This was the time when the **communists** started to rule the country.

Your friend,

John

P.S. Dad says that the rulers in China are changing the way the country is run. Southern China is close to Hong Kong, which is ruled by China now.

Glossary

Capital: The town or city where people who rule the country meet

Chopsticks: Two long sticks that are used for eating food. Both chopsticks are held between the fingers of one hand.

Clay: Earth, which can be shaped and fired to make things such as pots

Communists: People who think that everything in a country should be owned and shared by all the people who live there

Crops: Plants that farmers grow. Most crops are for food.

Emperor: A man who rules several different countries

Festival: A time when people celebrate something special or a special time of year

Goods: Things that can be sold

P.S.: This stands for Post Script. A postscript is the part of a card or letter that is added at the end, after the person has signed it.

Revolution: A complete change in the way a country is ruled

Steam locomotive: an engine that uses the power from steam to pull a train

Temple: A building where people go to pray

Terra-cotta: A kind of clay

Tomb: The place where a dead person is buried

Tourist: A person who is on vacation away from home

Index